How to Turn One Hundred Dollars into One Million Dollars in One Year

A Guide to Exponential Wealth Creation

Brian Michael Lawson

How to Turn One Hundred Dollars into One Million Dollars in One Year: A Guide to Exponential Wealth Creation

BRIAN MICHAEL LAWSON

Published by BRIAN MICHAEL LAWSON, 2023.

HOW TO TURN ONE HUNDRED DOLLARS INTO ONE MILLION DOLLARS IN ONE YEAR: A GUIDE TO EXPONENTIAL WEALTH CREATION

First edition. June 21, 2023.

Copyright © 2023 BRIAN MICHAEL LAWSON.

ISBN: 979-8215538128

Written by BRIAN MICHAEL LAWSON.

Also by BRIAN MICHAEL LAWSON

Thriving through Divorce: A Comprehensive Guide to Emotional, Personal, and Financial Recovery

The Memory of Water

La Memoria del Agua

¡Cómo convertir $100 en $1,000,000 en 1 año! Una guía para la creación de riqueza exponencial

Triunfando a Pesar del Divorcio: Una Guía Integral para la Recuperación Emocional, Personal y Financiera

Happily Ever After Is for You Too! A Guide to Never Giving Up Until You Find Your True Love

¡Y Fueron Felices Para Siempre también es para Ti! Una guía para nunca rendirse hasta encontrar tu amor verdadero

Mujeres Bellas Denegadas

Girls Disavowed

How to Turn One Hundred Dollars into One Million Dollars in One Year: A Guide to Exponential Wealth Creation

Table of Contents

Chapter 1: Introduction to Rapid Wealth Creation

1.1 Understanding the Mindset of Wealth Creation

To truly unlock the potential for rapid wealth creation, it is essential to cultivate the right mindset. In this chapter, let us embark on a journey of self-discovery as we explore the psychology behind wealth creation. By understanding the power of our thoughts and beliefs, we can pave the way for extraordinary financial success.

Positive thinking lies at the core of this transformative mindset. By embracing positivity, we transcend the limitations of scarcity thinking and open ourselves to a world of abundance. When we genuinely believe that opportunities are abundant and wealth is within our reach, we attract prosperity into our lives. This mindset shift empowers us to recognize and seize opportunities that may have otherwise gone unnoticed.

Self-belief, another crucial aspect, fuels our pursuit of wealth. It is the unwavering conviction in our abilities and the unwavering faith in our potential to achieve greatness. When we honestly believe in ourselves, we radiate confidence and attract the resources, partnerships, and circumstances that align with our aspirations. Through various techniques and practices, we will explore ways to strengthen our self-belief and eradicate self-doubt.

Visualization and affirmations play a pivotal role in shaping our mindset for wealth creation. By creating vivid mental images of our desired financial outcomes, we program our minds to seek and manifest those realities. Affirmations act as powerful statements that reinforce positive beliefs about us and our financial potential. Together, these practices enable us to align our thoughts, emotions, and actions with the vision of wealth we aspire to achieve.

Furthermore, embracing a visionary approach to wealth creation propels us beyond the confines of conventional thinking. It involves thinking big, setting audacious goals, and envisioning the impact we can make on the world. By embracing a larger purpose and aligning our financial goals with our values, we create a compelling driving force that fuels our determination and resilience in the face of challenges.

In this section, we have explored the foundational concepts that shape the mindset of wealth creation. By adopting an abundance mindset, cultivating self-belief, practicing visualization and affirmations, and embracing a visionary outlook, we equip ourselves with the tools necessary for rapid wealth creation. As we move forward, let us continue to delve deeper into the practical strategies and principles that will transform our dreams into tangible financial success.

Additionally, we explore the role of visualization and goal setting in wealth creation. By visualizing your desired outcomes and setting specific, measurable, attainable, relevant, and time-bound goals, you align your subconscious mind with your conscious actions. This powerful combination fuels your motivation and propels you forward on your wealth-building journey.

1.2 Setting Realistic Expectations and Goals

IN THE PURSUIT OF WEALTH creation, it is essential to set realistic expectations and goals that align with your individual aspirations. While the idea of rapid wealth accumulation may captivate our imagination, it is crucial to approach this endeavor with a realistic mindset. In this section, we emphasize the significance of establishing SMART goals – goals that are Specific, Measurable, Attainable, Relevant, and Time-bound.

By defining your financial goals with clarity and precision, you gain a clear vision of what you genuinely want to achieve. This vision becomes the guiding light that illuminates your path to success. It is essential to break down your overarching goals into smaller milestones, enabling you to track your progress and maintain motivation throughout the journey. This iterative approach allows you to celebrate achievements along the way, reinforcing your commitment and boosting your confidence.

Setting realistic expectations is not synonymous with settling for mediocrity. On the contrary, it is about understanding your starting point, recognizing the resources at your disposal, and acknowledging the time and effort required to attain your desired level of wealth. This approach empowers you to make informed decisions, take calculated risks, and remain steadfast in the face of challenges.

When you set realistic goals, you foster a sense of purpose and direction. Each milestone achieved serves as a steppingstone towards your ultimate vision. It is important to remain adaptable and open to adjusting your goals as circumstances evolve, ensuring that they remain relevant and attainable. Flexibility allows you to seize unexpected opportunities and navigate any detours along your wealth-building journey.

Moreover, realistic goal setting helps you avoid the pitfalls of unrealistic expectations. It shields you from the discouragement and disillusionment that can arise from overly ambitious objectives. By establishing achievable targets, you set yourself up for incremental progress and sustainable growth.

Remember, setting realistic expectations and goals does not imply complacency. It is about finding the delicate balance between ambition and feasibility, pushing your boundaries while staying grounded. By aligning your aspirations with a well-defined goal framework, you lay the foundation for long-term success. So, embark on this journey with a clear vision, tempered by a realistic mindset, and watch as your wealth grows steadily and abundantly.

1.3 Importance of Persistence and Adaptability

ACHIEVING FINANCIAL success and creating wealth is a journey filled with challenges and obstacles. In this section, we delve into the significance of persistence and adaptability in overcoming these inevitable hurdles. We passionately believe that with unwavering determination and a willingness to adapt, you can conquer any setback and continue on the path to prosperity.

Persistence is the driving force behind turning dreams into reality. It is the unwavering commitment to your goals, even when faced with difficulties or setbacks. It is the tenacity to push through obstacles, learn from failures, and keep moving forward. The road to wealth creation is rarely smooth, but persistence ensures that you stay focused and motivated, undeterred by temporary setbacks.

Consider the inspiring stories of those who have triumphed over adversity on their journey to financial success. From rags to riches, these individuals demonstrate the power of persistence. They faced countless rejections, encountered failures, and experienced moments of doubt. Yet, through their unwavering determination and refusal to give up, they eventually achieved remarkable success.

Adaptability is another crucial trait that complements persistence. In a constantly changing world, being adaptable allows you to navigate unforeseen circumstances and capitalize on new opportunities. It is the ability to adjust your strategies, embrace innovation, and pivot when necessary. By embracing change rather than resisting it, you position yourself to thrive in an ever-evolving financial landscape.

When challenges arise, it is important to assess the situation, learn from it, and adapt your approach accordingly. A certain investment strategy is not yielding the expected results, or a market shift requires a shift in your business model. Adapting to these changes enables you to stay ahead of the curve, identify emerging trends, and make informed decisions that lead to long-term success.

By incorporating persistence and adaptability into your wealth creation journey, you forge a path of resilience and growth. They provide you with the mindset and flexibility needed to overcome obstacles and seize opportunities. Remember, the road to wealth is not a linear one, but rather a series of peaks and valleys. It is your perseverance and adaptability that will determine your success.

So, as you embark on your journey to financial success, keep the flame of persistence burning bright within you. Embrace challenges as opportunities for growth and learning. Stay flexible, adapt to changing circumstances, and refine your strategies along the way. By embodying these qualities, you set yourself on a visionary path towards a future of abundance and fulfillment.

1.4 Strategies for Maximizing Limited Resources

EMBRACING THE CHALLENGE of limited resources is a hallmark of visionary entrepreneurs. It is not the lack of resources that determines success but the ability to leverage them wisely. In this chapter, we embark on a journey of innovation and resource optimization, discovering strategies to maximize every ounce of potential within your grasp.

1.4.1 Networking and Strategic Partnerships: The Power of Synergy

NO ONE ACHIEVES GREAT feats alone. By embracing the power of networking and building strategic partnerships, you unlock a realm of possibilities. Surround yourself with like-minded individuals, experts, and mentors who complement your skills and share your vision. Together, you can achieve more than you ever could on your own. Collaborate, pool your resources, and combine your strengths to create a win-win situation that propels you toward success. Remember, synergy fuels exponential growth.

1.4.2 Cost-Effective Marketing: Amplifying Your Impact on a Shoestring Budget

TRADITIONALLY, MARKETING has been associated with hefty budgets and big advertising campaigns. However, in the digital age, there are cost-effective avenues to make your mark without draining your coffers. Embrace the boundless potential of technology and digital platforms. Social media, content marketing, and targeted online advertising allow you to reach your specific audience with precision and efficiency. Craft compelling stories, share valuable insights, and engage with your audience authentically. By leveraging the power of the digital landscape, you can amplify your impact while keeping costs in check.

1.4.3 Thinking Creatively: Unleashing the Resourceful Visionary Within

RESOURCE CONSTRAINTS often ignite creativity. It is in moments of limitation that true innovation flourishes. Instead of dwelling on what you lack, focus on what you have at your disposal. Challenge conventional thinking, explore unconventional solutions, and reimagine possibilities. A visionary entrepreneur transcends the boundaries of conventional wisdom and finds innovative ways to leverage limited resources. Embrace the role of a resourceful visionary and discover the untapped potential within your reach.

1.4.4 Making the Most of Limited Resources: Practical Tips for Wealth Acceleration

WHILE A VISIONARY MINDSET is crucial, practical implementation is equally important. In this section, we provide you with practical tips and insights to make the most out of your limited resources. From leveraging outsourcing and automation to optimizing your time management and prioritizing tasks, we delve into the practical details of resource optimization. Discover how to allocate resources effectively, streamline processes, and eliminate inefficiencies. By becoming a Master of Resource Management, you unlock the key to accelerating your wealth-building journey.

In conclusion, limited resources should never hinder your quest for wealth creation. Instead, they should serve as a catalyst for innovation and resource optimization. Through networking and strategic partnerships, cost-effective marketing tactics, creative thinking, and practical implementation, you can maximize the potential of your limited resources. Embrace the challenges, adopt a visionary mindset, and let your resourcefulness shine as you embark on a transformative journey toward wealth creation.

1.5 Building a Strong Foundation for Financial

Success

IN THE PURSUIT OF FINANCIAL success, it is crucial to establish a strong foundation that can withstand the tests of time. This section delves into the essential elements required to build such a foundation, empowering you to achieve sustainable wealth creation.

Financial literacy serves as the bedrock of your journey towards prosperity. Understanding the principles of money management and familiarizing yourself with key concepts allows you to navigate the complex world of finance with confidence. By acquiring financial literacy, you gain the necessary tools to make informed decisions and seize opportunities that align with your goals.

A robust financial plan forms the cornerstone of your foundation. This plan takes into account your short-term and long-term objectives, providing a roadmap to guide your financial decisions. It acts as a compass, keeping you on track amidst the uncertainties of the market. Through careful planning and strategizing, you can optimize your resources and leverage them effectively to create wealth.

One crucial aspect of building a strong foundation is embracing the concept of multiple streams of income. Relying solely on a single income source can be precarious in an ever-changing economic landscape. By diversifying your income streams, you create resilience and enhance your financial stability. Exploring various avenues such as investments, side businesses, or passive income sources allows you to tap into additional revenue streams, increasing your overall earning potential.

Diversification extends beyond income sources and encompasses investments as well. A well-diversified investment portfolio mitigates risk by spreading your investments across different asset classes, sectors, and geographical regions. This approach reduces the impact of market volatility on your wealth and increases the likelihood of long-term growth. By diversifying, you position yourself to benefit from different economic cycles and capitalize on emerging opportunities.

Protecting your wealth is another critical aspect of building a strong foundation. Prudent investments and risk assessment play pivotal roles in safeguarding your financial well-being. Conducting thorough research and due diligence before making investment decisions ensures that your hard-earned money is directed towards ventures with favorable risk-return profiles. Adequate insurance coverage further shields you from unforeseen events that could otherwise jeopardize your financial stability.

By laying a solid foundation for financial success, you set the stage for long-term prosperity. This sturdy platform acts as a springboard from which your wealth can grow and flourish. It instills in you the confidence to weather economic storms and take calculated risks, knowing that you have a solid framework to rely upon. As your financial fortress strengthens, you gain the freedom and security to live life on your own terms, pursuing your passions, and fulfilling your aspirations.

Remember, building a strong foundation is an ongoing process that requires continuous learning, adaptation, and commitment. Embrace the power of knowledge, diversification, prudent investments, and risk management as you construct a solid financial base. By doing so, you pave the way for a future brimming with opportunities, financial well-being, and the ability to shape your own destiny.

Chapter 2: Leveraging the Power of Online Business

2.1 Identifying Lucrative Online Business Opportunities

Welcome to a world of boundless possibilities in the realm of online business. In this chapter, we embark on a journey of exploration, where we unravel emerging trends and unearth lucrative niches brimming with incredible growth potential. Get ready to immerse yourself in the art of market research, the intricate task of identifying target audiences, and the exhilarating process of selecting business models that harmonize perfectly with your passions and expertise.

As you delve deeper into this chapter, allow yourself to envision the exciting realm of online business opportunities unfurling right before your eyes. Picture the meteoric rise of e-commerce giants, the unstoppable surge of digital services, and the transformative power of virtual marketplaces. The digital landscape is an expansive canvas, awaiting your creative strokes to craft a masterpiece of success.

Market research becomes your guiding compass as you navigate this vast terrain. Dive into the intricacies of understanding consumer behavior, identifying their pain points, and anticipating their desires. Uncover the gaps in the market that present unique opportunities for innovative solutions. With each stroke of research, you gain a clearer vision of where your expertise and passion intersect with unmet needs.

Now, let us consider the concept of target audiences—the key protagonists in your entrepreneurial journey. Envision their diverse personas, their aspirations, and the challenges they face. Immerse yourself in their world to comprehend their motivations, preferences, and purchasing patterns. By aligning your offerings with their needs, you not only establish a deep connection but also unlock the potential for long-term customer loyalty and sustainable growth.

As you progress on this entrepreneurial odyssey, selecting the right business model takes center stage. Reflect on your personal strengths and interests, for they hold the power to fuel your business with unyielding enthusiasm. Will you create an e-commerce empire, captivating customers with a curated selection of products? Or will you leverage the digital landscape to offer transformative services that revolutionize industries? The choice is yours, but the key lies in choosing a path that ignites your passion and resonates with your vision.

Remember, in this exhilarating pursuit, no idea is too audacious, no dream too big. Allow your imagination to soar, for it is in the realms of audacity that the most revolutionary concepts are born. Cultivate an unwavering belief in your abilities, and let your vision guide your steps.

So, as we set foot on this path of identifying lucrative online business opportunities, open your mind to the endless possibilities that await. Embrace the transformative power of technology, the ever-evolving desires of consumers, and the limitless potential of your entrepreneurial spirit. Together, let us embark on this extraordinary journey of discovery, where success knows no bounds.

2.2 Creating a Profitable E-commerce Store

AMIDST THE DIGITAL revolution, the e-commerce realm has emerged as an unrivaled avenue for wealth creation. Allow us to be your guide as we navigate the path to establishing a profitable e-commerce store. Picture yourself sourcing or creating products that align with market demands and designing an online presence that captivates your audience.

In the vast landscape of e-commerce, success lies in understanding and mastering key concepts. Let us dive into some strategies and suggestions that can propel your e-commerce venture to new heights:

2.2.1 Effective Product Positioning

IMAGINE THE POWER OF strategically positioning your products to resonate with your target audience. By conducting market research, identifying gaps or trends, and analyzing consumer preferences, you can curate a product selection that speaks directly to the needs and desires of your customers. Consider offering unique features, solving specific problems, or catering to niche markets to set yourself apart from the competition.

2.2.2 Customer Acquisition

IN THE EVER-EXPANDING digital marketplace, acquiring customers is an essential component of your e-commerce success story. Visualize implementing various customer acquisition strategies, such as search engine optimization (SEO), pay-per-click (PPC) advertising, social media marketing, content marketing, and influencer collaborations. These approaches can help you generate targeted traffic to your online store, boost brand awareness, and convert visitors into loyal customers.

2.2.3 Conversion Optimization

IMAGINE THE IMPACT of optimizing your website or online store to increase the conversion rate. By analyzing user behavior, testing different layouts, improving website speed, and streamlining the purchasing process, you can enhance the user experience and encourage more visitors to make a purchase. Visualize employing persuasive copywriting, compelling product images, customer testimonials, and clear calls-to-action to instill trust and confidence in your potential buyers.

2.2.4 Embracing Emerging Technologies

IN TODAY'S RAPIDLY evolving digital landscape, staying ahead of the competition requires a visionary mindset and a willingness to embrace emerging technologies. By exploring the possibilities that these cutting-edge innovations offer, you can revolutionize the way you interact with customers and create unique experiences that set your e-commerce business apart. Let us delve into some key concepts and suggestions that can help you leverage emerging technologies to your advantage:

Envisioning the Future:

As a forward-thinking entrepreneur, it is essential to constantly envision the future of e-commerce. Imagine a world where your customers can seamlessly interact with your brand through advanced technologies, creating a personalized and immersive shopping experience. By tapping into your creativity and envisioning the possibilities, you can identify how emerging technologies can be integrated into your e-commerce ecosystem.

Integrating Chatbots and AI:

One way to enhance the customer experience and streamline operations is by integrating chatbots and AI-powered customer service tools. These intelligent virtual assistants can handle customer inquiries, provide product recommendations, and assist with order tracking, all in real-time. By leveraging chatbots, you can ensure 24/7 availability and instant support, delivering exceptional customer service and boosting customer satisfaction.

Unleashing the Power of Augmented Reality (AR) and Virtual Reality (VR):

Imagine if your customers could visualize your products in their own space before making a purchase. Augmented reality (AR) and virtual reality (VR) technologies enable just that. By creating immersive experiences, you can allow customers to interact with your products virtually, increasing engagement and reducing purchase hesitation. Whether it is trying on virtual clothes, visualizing furniture in their homes, or exploring destinations in a virtual travel experience, AR and VR can elevate your e-commerce business to new heights.

Staying Informed and Adaptive:

To fully embrace emerging technologies, it is crucial to stay informed about the latest innovations and trends in the e-commerce industry. Keep a close eye on industry publications, attend relevant conferences and events, and engage with technology thought leaders. By staying informed, you can identify new tools, platforms, or trends that align with your business objectives. Embrace a mindset of continuous learning and be ready to adapt and leverage new technologies as they emerge.

Collaborating and Partnering:

Emerging technologies often require specialized expertise and resources. Consider collaborating with technology partners or experts who can help you navigate the complex landscape of implementation and integration. Seek strategic alliances with companies specializing in AR/VR development, chatbot technologies, or AI solutions. By forming partnerships, you can leverage the expertise of others while focusing on your core business operations.

In conclusion, embracing emerging technologies is an exciting opportunity for e-commerce businesses to transform the customer experience and gain a competitive edge. By envisioning the future, integrating chatbots and AI, leveraging AR and VR, staying informed, and collaborating with experts, you can position your business at the forefront of innovation. Remember, the key to success lies in being open-minded, adaptable, and willing to explore the untapped potential that emerging technologies bring. Embrace the digital revolution and unlock new horizons for your e-commerce journey.

2.2.5 Building a Strong Brand

IN THE VAST SEA OF online stores, imagine the impact of building a strong and memorable brand. Invest time and effort in crafting a compelling brand story, developing a unique visual identity, and creating a consistent brand voice. Visualize establishing a strong online presence through engaging content, social media interactions, and personalized customer experiences. A well-defined brand can cultivate customer loyalty, encourage word-of-mouth marketing, and differentiate your e-commerce store from the competition.

As you embark on your journey to create a profitable e-commerce store, remember to envision the immense potential that lies within this dynamic and ever-evolving industry. By effectively positioning your products, acquiring customers through targeted strategies, optimizing conversions, embracing emerging technologies, and building a strong brand, you can set yourself on a path to e-commerce success.

Take inspiration from online guides and resources that provide step-by-step roadmaps to help you navigate the intricacies of establishing and growing an e-commerce business. Embrace your entrepreneurial spirit, stay adaptable, and seize the opportunities that the digital marketplace presents. Your vision, combined with diligent execution, has the power to turn your e-commerce store into a thriving and impactful enterprise.

2.3 Generating Passive Income through Affiliate Marketing

UNLOCK THE HIDDEN POTENTIAL of affiliate marketing and embark on a journey towards passive income generation. Imagine the power of leveraging your online platform to promote and sell products or services offered by others. Envision yourself as a trusted affiliate marketer, guiding your audience towards valuable solutions and reaping the rewards in return.

Within the realm of affiliate marketing, immerse yourself in strategies for building a loyal audience, selecting profitable affiliate programs, and optimizing conversions. Envision the streams of passive income flowing effortlessly into your life as you create a digital ecosystem that thrives on mutual trust and benefit. You can explore several options available on Amazon.com and other major online retailers and distributors.

2.4 Monetizing a Blog or Niche Website

UNLEASH THE FULL POTENTIAL of your creativity and passion through the art of blogging and niche websites. Envision yourself building a digital empire from the ground up, crafting captivating content that resonates with your target audience. Picture your blog or niche website as a hub of inspiration, information, and entertainment, drawing in a devoted following.

As we explore the process of monetization, envision multiple avenues opening before you. See the potential in display advertising, sponsored content, and selling digital products. Imagine driving hordes of eager readers to your platform, optimizing their user experience, and building a brand that leaves an indelible mark in their lives. Refer to the available format from the array of social medias available free options, which are plentiful to choose from.

2.5 Launching and Scaling a Successful Online Course

IN THIS RAPIDLY EVOLVING digital era, the demand for online education has reached unprecedented heights. Embrace the opportunity to create and launch your own online course, imparting your expertise to eager learners around the globe. Envision yourself as a beacon of knowledge, guiding individuals towards personal and professional growth through the power of online education.

Within the realm of online courses, envision the art of identifying a marketable skill, crafting meticulously structured course content, and designing engaging learning experiences. Picture the exhilaration of witnessing your course gain traction, attracting a multitude of students seeking to enhance their lives. Envision scaling your online course business to new heights, reaching audiences far and wide, and reaping the abundant rewards that come with transforming lives through education.

Let the motivational and visionary tone fuel your ambition. Embrace the specific concepts presented, each one offering a steppingstone towards your path of rapid wealth creation through online business ventures. Picture yourself as a trailblazer in the digital landscape, leaving a lasting legacy while realizing your financial dreams. The time is now to embark on this transformative journey and sculpt your own destiny in the realm of digital entrepreneurship.

Chapter 3: Exploring High-Potential Investment Ventures

We will embark on an exciting journey of exploring high-potential investment ventures. Investing wisely can be a powerful tool to grow your wealth and achieve financial freedom. By understanding the basics of investing and delving into specific investment avenues, we will equip you with the knowledge and insights needed to make informed investment decisions. Let us dive in!

3.1 Understanding the Basics of Investing

BEFORE VENTURING INTO specific investment opportunities, it is crucial to grasp the fundamentals of investing. We will explore key concepts such as risk and return, asset allocation, diversification, and the power of compounding. Understanding these principles will provide a solid foundation for your investment journey and enable you to make calculated decisions aligned with your financial goals.

3.1.1 Understanding Risk and return, Asset allocation, Diversification, and the Power of Compounding

RISK AND RETURN:

Risk refers to the uncertainty and potential for loss associated with an investment. It is possible that the actual return on an investment may differ from the expected return. Higher-risk investments offer the potential for higher returns, but they also carry a greater chance of loss. Return, on the other hand, represents the gain or profit generated from an investment over a specific period. It is the reward investors receive for taking on investment risk. The relationship between risk and return is typically positive, meaning that higher-risk investments have the potential for higher returns.

Asset Allocation:

Asset allocation refers to the process of distributing investment funds across different asset classes, such as stocks, bonds, real estate, and cash equivalents. It is based on the principle that different asset classes have varying levels of risk and return characteristics. By diversifying investments across multiple asset classes, investors aim to reduce overall risk and optimize potential returns. Asset allocation is typically determined based on an individual's risk tolerance, financial goals, and time horizon.

Diversification:

Diversification is a risk management strategy that involves spreading investments across different assets, industries, regions, or investment types. The goal of diversification is to reduce the impact of potential losses from any single investment or asset class. By diversifying a portfolio, investors can potentially offset losses in one investment with gains in others. Diversification helps to mitigate risk and increase the likelihood of achieving more consistent and stable returns over time.

The Power of Compounding:

The power of compounding refers to the ability of an investment to generate earnings on both the initial principal and the accumulated interest or returns over time. As investment returns are reinvested, the compounding effect magnifies the growth of the investment. Over a long period, compounding can lead to exponential growth. The key to maximizing the power of compounding is to start investing early, reinvest earnings, and maintain a long-term investment horizon. By harnessing the power of compounding, even small investments can grow significantly over time and contribute to long-term wealth accumulation.

3.2 Investing in Stocks and Dividend-Yielding Companies

STOCK MARKET INVESTING offers great potential for wealth creation. We will delve into the world of stocks, exploring how to evaluate companies, analyze financial statements, and identify undervalued stocks with growth potential. Try to focus on dividend-yielding companies, which provide a passive income stream through regular dividend payments. Learn strategies to identify companies with sustainable dividends and unlock the potential of long-term wealth accumulation.

3.3 Real Estate Investment Strategies for Quick Returns

REAL ESTATE INVESTMENT can be a lucrative avenue for generating quick returns. We will examine different strategies such as flipping properties, rental investments, and real estate crowdfunding. Discover online guides on how to conduct market research, evaluate property value, negotiate deals, and manage your real estate portfolio effectively. Uncover the secrets to building wealth through real estate and capitalize on the opportunities available in this dynamic market.

3.3.1 Understanding Flipping Properties, Rental Investments, and Real Estate Crowdfunding

FLIPPING PROPERTIES:

Flipping properties refers to the practice of purchasing a property, typically at a discounted price, with the intention of renovating or improving it and selling it at a higher price in a relatively short period. Flippers often focus on distressed properties or those in need of significant repairs. The goal is to add value to the property through renovations or upgrades and then quickly sell it for a profit.

Rental Investments:

Rental investments involve purchasing properties with the intention of generating income by renting them out to tenants. Investors can acquire residential properties (such as houses, apartments, or condominiums) or commercial properties (such as office spaces or retail units). Rental investments offer the potential for ongoing cash flow and long-term wealth accumulation. Investors typically earn rental income that exceeds their expenses (such as mortgage payments, property taxes, and maintenance costs) and may also benefit from property appreciation over time.

Real Estate Crowdfunding:

Real estate crowdfunding is a new investment model that allows multiple investors to pool their funds together to invest in real estate projects. Through online platforms, individual investors can access a wide range of real estate opportunities, including residential, commercial, or industrial properties, without the need for substantial capital. Investors can choose specific projects based on their preferences and risk appetite. In return for their investment, they typically receive returns in the form of rental income, capital appreciation, or profit-sharing, depending on the structure of the investment and the project's success. Real estate crowdfunding provides an avenue for individuals to participate in real estate investments with lower barriers to entry and potentially diversify their portfolios.

3.3.2 Market Research and Evaluation: Unveiling the Path to Real Estate Success

IN THE VAST REALM OF real estate investment, knowledge is power. To unlock the doors of success, you must embark on a journey of comprehensive market research and property evaluation. By delving into the depths of these essential concepts, you will gain a profound understanding of market dynamics, seize opportunities, and maximize your returns on investment. Let us explore the key aspects of market research and evaluation, and how they can propel your real estate ventures to new heights.

3.3.2.1 Market Research: Illuminating Insights into Local Dynamics

TO MAKE INFORMED INVESTMENT decisions, it is imperative to comprehend the intricate tapestry of local market trends. Dive deep into the nuances of your target location, unraveling the shifting dynamics that shape the real estate landscape. Analyze the pulse of the market, studying factors such as supply and demand, rental rates, vacancy rates, and property appreciation trends. By immersing yourself in this wealth of information, you can anticipate market fluctuations, identify emerging opportunities, and align your investments with the zeitgeist of the moment.

3.3.2.2 Demographic Shifts: The Foundation of Investment Wisdom

A VISIONARY REAL ESTATE investor recognizes the immense impact of demographic shifts on property demand and value. Unearth the ever-changing tides of population growth, migration patterns, and urban development. Understand the needs and aspirations of the communities that surround your potential investments. By staying attuned to these demographic changes, you can position yourself strategically, meeting the demands of a dynamic market and unlocking the doors to sustainable success.

3.3.2.3 Economic Indicators: Decoding the Symphony of Prosperity

AS A SHREWD INVESTOR, you must learn to decipher the symphony of economic indicators that influence real estate markets. Delve into the depths of economic data, examining factors such as employment rates, GDP growth, inflation, and interest rates. Understand the symbiotic relationship between the economy and the real estate sector. By harnessing this knowledge, you can anticipate market trends, identify optimal investment opportunities, and navigate the currents of prosperity with confidence.

3.3.2.4 Property Evaluation: Unveiling the Gems Amongst the Dust

IN THE REALM OF REAL estate investment, a discerning eye for property evaluation is your compass. Cultivate the expertise to assess the value and potential of prospective properties. Acquire the tools to evaluate location, amenities, property condition, and market demand. Unearth the hidden gems amidst a sea of possibilities, selecting properties that align harmoniously with your investment objectives. With every investment, aim to uncover the untapped potential and envision the transformation that lies within.

3.3.2.5 Unleashing the Power of Online Resources and Expert Guidance

IN THIS DIGITAL AGE, a vast array of resources and expert guidance awaits at your fingertips. Harness the power of online platforms, guides, and expert advice to augment your market research and evaluation endeavors. Immerse yourself in industry insights, absorb expert opinions, and learn from those who have walked the path before you. Embrace the wisdom shared by seasoned professionals, distilling their knowledge to craft your unique investment strategies.

3.3.2.6 Embrace the Journey of Real Estate Mastery

THE PURSUIT OF REAL estate investment success is an ongoing journey, filled with endless opportunities for growth and prosperity. Embrace the thrill of market research and evaluation as vital pillars of your investment strategy. Equip yourself with the tools, insights, and visionary mindset required to navigate the ever-changing currents of the real estate market. With each investment decision, let your knowledge guide you, and your passion drive you towards a future defined by limitless possibilities.

3.4 Venturing into Cryptocurrencies and Blockchain Technology:

CRYPTOCURRENCIES AND blockchain technology have unleashed a wave of innovation that is reshaping the financial landscape as we know it. In this section, we embark on an exciting journey to uncover the fundamentals of cryptocurrencies and delve into the transformative power of blockchain technology.

We start by unraveling the intricate world of cryptocurrencies, from the pioneering Bitcoin to the vast array of digital currencies that have emerged since. You will grasp the underlying principles of decentralized digital currencies, exploring concepts such as cryptography, distributed ledger technology, and consensus algorithms. By understanding these foundational elements, you will gain a solid grasp of how cryptocurrencies operate and their potential implications.

But the story does not end there. We delve deeper into blockchain technology, the groundbreaking innovation behind cryptocurrencies. Blockchain represents a paradigm shift in how we validate and store data securely. Its distributed and transparent nature eliminates the need for intermediaries, fostering trust and efficiency across a wide range of industries. Discover how blockchain can disrupt sectors such as finance, supply chain management, healthcare, and more.

As we navigate the thrilling world of cryptocurrencies and blockchain, we also shed light on the risks and considerations associated with this emerging asset class. Volatility and regulatory challenges pose unique obstacles, demanding a cautious approach. You will gain insights into strategies to mitigate risks, protect your investments, and make informed decisions in this fast-paced and dynamic ecosystem.

Additionally, we explore investment opportunities within cryptocurrencies. By examining market trends, evaluating project fundamentals, and understanding the intricacies of token economics, you will be equipped to identify potential gems amidst the sea of digital assets. We emphasize the importance of conducting thorough research and due diligence before committing your resources, empowering you to navigate the ever-evolving landscape of cryptocurrencies with confidence.

This section aims to equip you with the knowledge and tools needed to venture into the captivating world of cryptocurrencies and blockchain technology. By grasping the fundamentals, assessing risks, and identifying opportunities, you will position yourself to seize the transformative potential of this rapidly evolving digital frontier.

3.5 Assessing High-Growth Startups and Angel Investing Opportunities:

THE WORLD OF HIGH-GROWTH startups and angel investing beckons those with a vision for the future and a hunger for extraordinary returns. In this section, we embark on a thrilling exploration of the entrepreneurial landscape, uncovering the secrets of identifying promising startups and engaging in angel investing.

We start by immersing ourselves in the mindset of successful angel investors, visionaries who have supported some of the most disruptive and game-changing companies of our time. Drawing inspiration from their experiences, we unlock the key attributes they look for in potential investment opportunities. From market potential and scalability to the strength of the founding team, you will gain a comprehensive understanding of what sets high-growth startups apart.

As we continue our journey, we delve into the art of due diligence—the meticulous process of assessing startups and their growth potential. We dissect the critical elements that demand scrutiny, from market analysis and competitive landscapes to financial projections and intellectual property evaluation. Armed with these insights, you will be empowered to make informed investment decisions, identifying startups that possess the potential to soar to unprecedented heights.

We also shed light on the risks inherent in angel investing. Early-stage companies face numerous challenges, and not all will emerge victorious. We explore strategies to mitigate risk and safeguard your investments, including diversification, building a robust portfolio, and seeking expert advice when necessary. By understanding the pitfalls and how to navigate them, you will be well-prepared to embark on this exciting and rewarding investment journey.

But it is not solely about the financial rewards. Engaging in angel investing allows you to be a catalyst for change, supporting innovative ideas that have the power to reshape industries and improve lives. By nurturing promising startups, you contribute to the fabric of entrepreneurship, fostering an ecosystem that drives progress and innovation.

In this section, we encourage you to envision yourself as a patron of the next generation of disruptors. Through angel investing, you have the opportunity to participate in their journey, share their triumphs, and potentially multiply your investment manifold. It is an exhilarating path that requires both strategic thinking and a daring spirit, but the rewards can be immeasurable.

The reader is encouraged to explore the world of high-growth startups and angel investing, where visionary minds converge to support groundbreaking ideas. Unleash your inner entrepreneur, assess opportunities with a discerning eye, and prepare to embark on an investment journey that goes beyond financial gains. Together, let us shape the future and leave an indelible mark on the world of innovation.

Conclusion:

In this chapter, we have embarked on an exploration of high-potential investment ventures. Understanding the basics of investing, diving into stocks and dividend-yielding companies, exploring real estate investment strategies, venturing into cryptocurrencies and blockchain technology, and assessing high-growth startups and angel investing opportunities are all pathways to wealth creation. By applying the knowledge and concepts discussed in this chapter, you can position yourself to capitalize on lucrative investment opportunities and unlock the potential for significant financial growth. Remember, with informed decision-making and a visionary mindset, you can navigate the investment landscape and embark on a journey toward financial prosperity.

Chapter 4: Tapping into the Sharing Economy

In this chapter, we will explore the transformative power of the sharing economy and how you can capitalize on its various facets to generate passive income and unlock new opportunities. The sharing economy has revolutionized traditional industries by leveraging technology and empowering individuals to monetize their assets, skills, and time. By embracing the principles of sharing and collaboration, you can tap into this dynamic ecosystem and embark on a journey towards financial freedom and flexibility.

4.1 Capitalizing on the Ride-Sharing Revolution

THE RISE OF RIDE-SHARING platforms such as Uber and Lyft have disrupted the transportation industry and created unprecedented opportunities for individuals to generate passive income. By becoming a ride-share driver, you can leverage your vehicle to earn money during your spare time. This concept not only provides an additional revenue stream but also allows you to maximize the value of your car and reduce the overall cost of ownership. With the freedom to set your own schedule and the potential for lucrative incentives, the ride-sharing revolution can be a steppingstone towards achieving your financial goals.

Key Concepts:

- Ride-sharing platforms as a source of passive income.
- Flexible schedule and potential incentives.
- Maximizing the value of your vehicle.

4.2 Renting Assets for Passive Income

THE SHARING ECONOMY extends beyond transportation, presenting opportunities to monetize other assets such as property and vehicles. By renting out your spare rooms or entire properties through platforms like Airbnb, you can tap into the growing demand for unique and personalized accommodation experiences. This approach allows you to leverage your property investment and generate a consistent stream of passive income. Similarly, platforms like Turo enable you to rent out your underutilized vehicles, turning them into revenue-generating assets. Renting assets not only provides a passive income stream but also maximizes the utilization of your resources.

Key Concepts:
- Renting out spare rooms or properties through Airbnb.
- Leveraging property investments for passive income.
- Monetizing underutilized vehicles with platforms like Turo.

4.3 Participating in the Gig Economy

THE GIG ECONOMY OFFERS a range of flexible, task-based job opportunities that allow individuals to monetize their skills and expertise. By becoming a freelancer or engaging in task-based jobs, you can gain control over your time, choose projects that align with your passions, and build a diverse portfolio of clients. Platforms like Upwork, Fiverr, and TaskRabbit connect freelancers with businesses and individuals seeking specific services. Whether you possess writing, design, programming, or consulting skills, the gig economy enables you to unlock your entrepreneurial potential and generate passive income by leveraging your expertise.

Key Concepts:
- Flexible, task-based job opportunities in the gig economy.
- Monetizing skills and expertise as a freelancer.
- Platforms connecting freelancers with clients.

4.4 Building a Successful Airbnb Rental Business

IF YOU ASPIRE TO TAKE your passive income from property rentals to the next level, building a successful Airbnb rental business can be a lucrative endeavor. This section explores the strategies and best practices for creating a remarkable guest experience, optimizing occupancy rates, and maximizing rental income. From interior design and effective listing management to guest communication and hospitality, you will gain insights into the key factors that contribute to Airbnb success. By delivering exceptional experiences, securing positive reviews, and continuously refining your operations, you can build a sustainable and profitable Airbnb rental business.

Key Concepts:

- Strategies for creating a remarkable guest experience.

- Optimizing occupancy rates and rental income.

- Best practices in listing management and guest communication.

4.5 Exploring Opportunities in the Peer-to-Peer Lending Market

THE PEER-TO-PEER LENDING market offers an alternative investment avenue for individuals seeking to earn passive income. By participating in this growing sector, you can act as a lender, providing loans to individuals or small businesses through online platforms. This approach allows you to diversify your investment portfolio and earn interest on the funds you lend. While there are risks involved, proper due diligence and understanding the lending platforms can mitigate potential pitfalls. Exploring the opportunities in the peer-to-peer lending market enables you to contribute to the financial well-being of borrowers while generating passive income for yourself.

Key Concepts:

- Peer-to-peer lending as an alternative investment avenue.

- Diversifying investment portfolio through lending.
- Conducting due diligence and managing risks.

Conclusion:

Tapping into the sharing economy presents an array of opportunities to generate passive income and embrace the changing landscape of work and entrepreneurship. By capitalizing on the ride-sharing revolution, renting assets, participating in the gig economy, building a successful Airbnb rental business, and exploring the peer-to-peer lending market, you can unlock new sources of income and achieve financial freedom. Embrace the principles of sharing, collaboration, and leveraging technology to embark on a rewarding journey towards a more flexible and prosperous future.

Chapter 5: Unleashing Entrepreneurial Creativity

5.1 Identifying a Profitable Niche or Gap in the Market

In this chapter, we delve into the exciting realm of entrepreneurial creativity, where innovative ideas and strategic thinking meet profitability. Identifying a profitable niche or gap in the market is the first step towards launching a successful business venture. We will explore how to tap into your creativity and identify unique opportunities that have the potential to disrupt industries and captivate customers.

We start by guiding you through a process of market research and analysis. By studying market trends, consumer behavior, and emerging needs, you will gain valuable insights into unmet demands and untapped markets. We encourage you to think beyond the obvious and search for gaps that others may have overlooked.

Next, we provide practical tools and techniques for idea generation and evaluation. Drawing on proven brainstorming methods and creative exercises, you will learn how to unlock your imagination and generate innovative business concepts. We emphasize the importance of validating your ideas through market testing and customer feedback to ensure viability and potential profitability.

To illustrate these concepts, we share real-life success stories of entrepreneurs who identified untapped niches and capitalized on them. From tech startups disrupting traditional industries to niche product businesses catering to specific customer segments, these inspiring examples will ignite your entrepreneurial spirit and encourage you to think outside the box.

By the end of this chapter, you will have the tools and mindset necessary to identify a profitable niche or gap in the market. Armed with creativity and market knowledge, you will be ready to embark on your entrepreneurial journey and make a meaningful impact in your chosen industry.

5.2 Launching a Small-Scale Manufacturing Business

IN THIS SECTION, WE explore the exciting world of small-scale manufacturing and how it can be a pathway to entrepreneurial success. We delve into the step-by-step process of launching a manufacturing business from scratch, even with limited resources.

We begin by highlighting the advantages and opportunities of small-scale manufacturing. From the ability to control quality and customization to leveraging local sourcing and reducing operational costs, we emphasize the unique benefits that small-scale manufacturing offers in today's market.

Next, we guide you through the crucial steps of setting up your manufacturing business. We cover aspects such as sourcing raw materials, selecting suitable production methods, designing efficient workflows, and implementing quality control measures. We emphasize the importance of meticulous planning, strategic partnerships, and embracing technological advancements to optimize efficiency and ensure a competitive edge.

Furthermore, we address the challenges you may encounter in the manufacturing industry and provide strategies to overcome them. Whether it is managing production costs, navigating regulatory requirements, or building a skilled workforce, we offer practical advice and insights from experienced entrepreneurs who have successfully overcome similar obstacles.

By the end of this section, you will have a comprehensive understanding of how to launch a small-scale manufacturing business. Equipped with the knowledge and practical tips provided, you will be empowered to turn your entrepreneurial dreams into reality and establish a thriving manufacturing enterprise.

5.3 Franchising as a Shortcut to Business Success

FRANCHISING IS AN AVENUE that offers aspiring entrepreneurs a shortcut to business success. In this section, we explore the world of franchising and its immense potential for those looking for a proven business model and a faster route to profitability.

We start by examining the benefits of franchising, highlighting how it allows entrepreneurs to leverage established brand recognition, operational systems, and marketing strategies. You will learn how franchising can significantly reduce the risks typically associated with starting a new business, as well as expedite the learning curve by providing comprehensive training and ongoing support.

We delve into the step-by-step process of becoming a franchisee. From researching and selecting the right franchise opportunity to negotiating contracts and securing financing, we provide a comprehensive roadmap to guide you through the entire franchising journey. We emphasize the importance of due diligence and conducting thorough investigations to ensure alignment with your personal and financial goals.

Additionally, we address the responsibilities and challenges that come with owning a franchise. We discuss the importance of maintaining brand standards, managing customer expectations, and fostering strong relationships with franchisors and fellow franchisees. By sharing real-life success stories and lessons learned, we provide valuable insights into the day-to-day realities of running a franchised business.

By the end of this section, you will have a deep understanding of the franchising model and the steps required to become a successful franchisee. Armed with this knowledge, you will be empowered to make informed decisions, identify lucrative franchise opportunities, and embark on a journey towards entrepreneurial prosperity.

5.4 Creating and Monetizing Intellectual Property (e.g., Patents, Trademarks)

IN THIS SEGMENT, WE explore the fascinating realm of intellectual property (IP) and its potential for creating substantial wealth. We dive into the world of patents, trademarks, copyrights, and trade secrets, uncovering the power of IP in driving business success and generating passive income.

We begin by providing a comprehensive overview of different types of intellectual property and their respective benefits and protection mechanisms. You will gain a solid understanding of the legal frameworks surrounding IP and learn how to safeguard your creations and ideas from unauthorized use.

Next, we delve into the process of creating and monetizing intellectual property. We explore effective strategies for identifying valuable ideas and innovations, conducting prior art searches, and filing patent applications. We also discuss the importance of trademark registration to protect your brand identity and distinguish your products or services in the market.

Furthermore, we shed light on the various avenues for monetizing intellectual property. From licensing and franchising to strategic partnerships and royalties, we provide insights into different revenue streams that can turn your intellectual creations into profitable assets. We offer guidance on negotiation techniques, contract drafting, and ongoing management of IP assets.

By the end of this section, you will be equipped with the knowledge and tools necessary to navigate the intricacies of intellectual property creation and monetization. Whether you are an inventor, artist, or creative entrepreneur, you will discover how to protect your valuable creations and leverage them to build a thriving business empire.

5.5 Scaling a Service-Based Business for Rapid Growth

IN THIS FINAL SEGMENT, we explore the art of scaling a service-based business for rapid growth. We unveil the strategies and principles that successful service entrepreneurs have employed to expand their ventures and maximize their impact in the market.

We start by discussing the importance of building a strong foundation for scalability. From developing standardized processes and systems to recruiting and training a competent team, we emphasize the significance of establishing a solid infrastructure that can support rapid growth.

In the next section we delve into effective marketing and sales strategies for service-based businesses. We explore digital marketing techniques, referral programs, strategic partnerships, and other growth-focused initiatives that can help you attract new clients and expand your customer base. We emphasize the role of customer satisfaction and referral marketing in fueling exponential growth.

Furthermore, we addressed the operational challenges that accompany rapid scaling and offer practical solutions to overcome them. From managing increased workloads and maintaining service quality to optimizing productivity and implementing automation, we provided insights and best practices for handling the complexities of a growing service-based enterprise.

With a little trial and error using the roadmap provided in this chapter, you will possess the knowledge and strategies necessary to scale your service-based business for rapid growth. Armed with the principles shared and real-life case studies, you will be empowered to expand your operations, increase profitability, and establish yourself as a leader in your industry.

5.6 Fueling Growth Through Dynamic Marketing and Sales Strategies

IN THE DYNAMIC WORLD of service-based businesses, effective marketing and sales strategies play a pivotal role in driving growth, attracting new clients, and solidifying your position as a leader in your industry. In this subsection, we delve into the exciting realm of marketing and sales for service entrepreneurs, providing you with motivational insights and detail-oriented tactics to fuel your business's success.

5.6.1. Develop a Compelling Brand Identity

YOUR BRAND IS THE ESSENCE of your service-based business. Invest time and energy in crafting a compelling brand identity that resonates with your target audience. Define your unique value proposition, mission, and brand personality. Create a captivating brand story that evokes emotion and establishes a strong connection with potential clients.

5.6.2. Craft a Stellar Online Presence

IN TODAY'S DIGITAL age, a strong online presence is non-negotiable. Build a visually appealing and user-friendly website that showcases your services, expertise, and client success stories. Optimize your website for search engines to ensure maximum visibility. Leverage social media platforms to engage with your audience, share valuable content, and build a community of loyal followers.

5.6.3. Harness the Power of Content Marketing

POSITION YOURSELF AS an industry thought leader by consistently creating and sharing high-quality, informative content. Publish insightful blog posts, create engaging videos, and offer downloadable resources that address your target audience's pain points. Be generous with your knowledge and expertise, establishing yourself as the go-to authority in your niche.

5.6.4. Embrace the Art of Storytelling

STORIES HAVE THE POWER to captivate and inspire. Share compelling stories that showcase the transformative impact your services have had on clients' lives. Craft case studies and testimonials that highlight the unique value you bring to the table. Use storytelling to create an emotional connection with your prospects, making them eager to experience the transformation you provide.

5.6.5. Leverage Referral Marketing

WORD-OF-MOUTH REFERRALS are a powerful marketing tool for service-based businesses. Delight your existing clients by exceeding their expectations and providing exceptional service. Encourage satisfied clients to refer you to their network by implementing referral programs, offering incentives, or simply asking for referrals. Positive testimonials and personal recommendations can significantly boost your credibility and attract new clients.

5.6.6. Cultivate Strategic Partnerships

COLLABORATE WITH COMPLEMENTARY service providers and industry influencers to expand your reach and tap into new client bases. Seek out potential partners who share your target audience and have a similar ethos. Collaborate on joint marketing campaigns, co-host webinars, or participate in industry events together. Strategic partnerships can provide access to new markets and establish you as a trusted authority within your industry.

5.6.7. Embrace Digital Advertising

SUPPLEMENT YOUR ORGANIC marketing efforts with targeted digital advertising campaigns. Utilize platforms like Google Ads, social media advertising, or content syndication to reach a broader audience and drive traffic to your website. Set clear goals for your advertising campaigns, refine your targeting parameters, and track your results meticulously to optimize your return on investment.

5.6.8. Nurture Personal Connection

IN THE SERVICE INDUSTRY, building personal connections is key. Attending industry conferences, networking events, and trade shows to establish face-to-face connections with potential clients and industry influencers. Cultivate relationships by actively listening, offering support, and providing value to others. Genuine connections can lead to long-term partnerships and a steady stream of referrals.

5.6.9. Prioritize Exceptional Customer Service

DELIVER AN OUTSTANDING customer experience at every touchpoint. Provide prompt responses to inquiries, go the extra mile to exceed expectations, and personalize your interactions. Happy clients become loyal advocates who not only return for repeat business but also refer others to your services.

5.6.10. Continuously Monitor and Optimize

MARKETING AND SALES strategies evolve, and it is crucial to stay agile and adaptive. Regularly monitor your marketing efforts, track key performance indicators, and gather customer feedback. Analyze data to identify what's working and what needs improvement. Experiment with new strategies, discard underperforming tactics, and embrace innovative approaches to stay ahead of the competition.

Remember, the combination of passion, authenticity, and strategic marketing and sales efforts is the recipe for success in the service-based business world. Harness your entrepreneurial spirit, embrace these dynamic strategies, and watch your business thrive as you connect with clients, make a positive impact, and achieve your vision of success.

Conclusion of Chapter 5: our book embarked on an energetic and visionary journey into the realm of entrepreneurial creativity. This guide provides detailed insights and actionable steps for identifying profitable niches which can apply to launching small-scale manufacturing businesses, leveraging franchising, creating, and monetizing intellectual property, and scaling service-based enterprises.

With a motivational tone and a focus on practical details, we guide aspiring entrepreneurs to unlock their creative potential and achieve extraordinary success. Whether you are seeking innovative business ideas, shortcuts to success, or strategies for growth, this chapter equips you with the knowledge and mindset necessary to make your entrepreneurial dreams a reality.

Embrace the power of entrepreneurial creativity, seize lucrative opportunities, and pave your own path towards a thriving and fulfilling business venture. The possibilities are endless, and the journey awaits you.

Chapter 6: Navigating the World of Passive Income Streams

6.1 Building a Dividend Portfolio for Long-Term Wealth Creation:

In this chapter, we embark on a journey towards long-term wealth creation through the power of dividend investing. Imagine receiving regular cash payments from your investments while your wealth grows steadily. Building a dividend portfolio is a proven strategy to achieve just that.

By carefully selecting dividend-paying stocks from stable and reputable companies, you can create a stream of passive income that continues to flow even when you sleep. Companies that consistently distribute dividends demonstrate their commitment to sharing profits with shareholders.

We will explore the art of identifying high-quality dividend stocks that offer a balance between yield and sustainability. Through detailed analysis and research, we will uncover the key factors to consider when selecting dividend stocks, such as the company's financial health, dividend history, and growth potential.

6.2 Generating Rental Income through Real Estate Properties:

UNLOCK THE POTENTIAL of real estate as a passive income stream in this chapter. Discover the lucrative world of rental properties, where your money works for you while tenants pay off your mortgage and provide a steady stream of income.

We will delve into the fundamentals of real estate investment, including property selection, financing options, and property management strategies. From single-family homes to apartment complexes, you will learn how to identify properties with strong rental demand, negotiate favorable deals, and maximize your rental income.

6.3 Designing and Selling Digital Products (eBooks, Courses):

WELCOME TO THE DIGITAL age, where the creation and sale of digital products open up endless possibilities for passive income. In this chapter, we explore the world of digital entrepreneurship, empowering you to share your knowledge and expertise with the world while generating income on autopilot.

We will guide you through the process of creating captivating eBooks, transformative online courses, and other digital products that cater to your audience's needs. From ideation to content creation, marketing strategies, and sales funnels, you will learn how to develop a digital product empire that generates passive income even while you sleep.

6.4 Maximizing Returns from Peer-to-Peer Lending Platforms:

PREPARE TO REVOLUTIONIZE your understanding of lending and borrowing in this chapter. Peer-to-peer lending platforms offer a remarkable opportunity to earn passive income by lending money directly to individuals or businesses.

We will navigate the world of peer-to-peer lending, exploring the platforms, assessing risk factors, and identifying strategies to maximize your returns. You will learn how to evaluate borrower profiles, diversify your lending portfolio, and mitigate potential risks while enjoying the benefits of consistent interest payments.

6.5 Exploring Royalty Opportunities in Creative Industries:

UNLEASH YOUR CREATIVE potential and explore the world of royalties in this captivating chapter. If you possess artistic talents or have a passion for creative endeavors, there are opportunities to monetize your work and earn passive income through royalties.

From writing books and composing music to creating artwork and designing innovative products, we will uncover the avenues available for artists, authors, and inventors to generate ongoing royalties. You will learn how to protect your intellectual property, negotiate favorable royalty agreements, and tap into various distribution channels.

Following the guidelines presented in the chapter, you will unlock the secrets to navigating the world of passive income streams. Whether through dividend investing, real estate properties, digital products, peer-to-peer lending, or royalty opportunities, you will discover the pathways to financial freedom and a life of abundance. Embrace the opportunities that lie ahead and embark on your journey to passive wealth creation.

Chapter 7: Strategies for Financial Optimization

7.1 Implementing Effective Budgeting and Money Management Techniques

In this chapter, we dive deep into the world of effective budgeting and money management techniques that can transform your financial situation. We explore practical strategies to help you take control of your finances and achieve your goals.

Imagine a life where you no longer worry about living paycheck to paycheck, where you have a clear understanding of your income and expenses, and where you confidently allocate your resources to align with your priorities. This is the power of effective budgeting and money management.

We begin by outlining step-by-step methods to create a budget that works for you. We provide real-life examples of budgeting templates and tools that you can easily adapt to your own needs. By tracking your income and expenses meticulously, you will gain a deep understanding of your spending habits and identify areas where you can make adjustments to save more and spend wisely.

7.2 Minimizing Debt and Maximizing Savings

DEBT CAN BE A HEAVY burden that restricts your financial freedom and prevents you from achieving your dreams. In this section, we uncover powerful strategies to minimize debt and maximize your savings, propelling you towards a future of financial security and abundance.

We delve into proven techniques for paying off debt efficiently, such as the snowball or avalanche method, providing clear examples and case studies. You will learn how to prioritize your debts, negotiate with creditors, and develop a repayment plan that works for your unique circumstances.

Moreover, we explore various methods to build your savings effectively. From setting up automatic transfers to implementing the **50/30/20 rule**, we offer actionable advice that will help you establish an emergency fund, save for future goals, and create a strong financial foundation. In the next subsection this 50/30/20 rule is explained.

7.2.1 The 50/30/20 Rule

THE 50/20/30 RULE IS a simple budgeting guideline that helps individuals allocate their income effectively to achieve financial balance. It suggests dividing your after-tax income into three main categories: needs, savings, and wants. Here is how the rule breaks down:

1. 50% for Needs:

Allocate 50% of your after-tax income to cover essential needs and obligations. This category includes expenses such as:

- Rent or mortgage payments
- Utilities (electricity, water, gas)
- Groceries and essential food items
- Health insurance premiums
- Transportation costs (car payments, public transportation, fuel)
- Minimum debt payments (credit cards, loans)

By dedicating 50% of your income to cover these necessary expenses, you ensure that your basic needs are met and maintain financial stability.

2. 20% for Savings:

Devote 20% of your income to savings and financial goals. This category includes:

- Emergency fund contributions
- Retirement savings (401(k), IRA, pension plans)
- Investments
- Debt repayment (above the minimum required payment)
- Saving for future expenses (down payment for a house, education funds)

By prioritizing savings, you establish a strong financial foundation and work towards long-term financial security and goals.

3. 30% for Wants:

Allocate 30% of your income for discretionary spending and wants. This category includes non-essential expenses such as:

- Dining out and entertainment
- Travel and vacations
- Shopping and hobbies
- Subscription services (streaming, gym memberships)
- Personal care and luxury items

The 30% category allows you to enjoy your income and indulge in discretionary expenses without compromising your financial stability.

It is important to note that the 50/20/30 rule is a guideline and can be adjusted based on individual circumstances and priorities. For example, if you have significant debt, you may choose to allocate more towards debt repayment, reducing the percentage for wants temporarily. The key is to find a balance that aligns with your financial goals and helps you make intentional decisions about your money.

By following the 50/20/30 rule, you can develop healthy financial habits, effectively manage your income, and work towards a secure financial future.

7.3 Tax Planning and Strategies for Wealth Preservation

TAXES CAN SIGNIFICANTLY impact your financial well-being, but with the right knowledge and strategies, you can optimize your tax situation and preserve your hard-earned wealth. In this section, we provide you with a comprehensive understanding of tax planning and offer practical tips to minimize your tax liability while remaining compliant with tax laws.

We illustrate how various tax deductions and credits can work in your favor, and we guide you through the process of tax-efficient investing. You will gain insights into tax-advantaged accounts, such as IRAs and 401(k)s, and learn how to leverage them to grow your wealth while reducing your tax burden.

With our visionary approach, we empower you to take charge of your taxes and proactively plan for a prosperous financial future.

7.4 Leveraging Technology for Financial Efficiency

IN THIS DIGITAL AGE, technology offers immense potential to streamline your financial management and enhance your financial efficiency. We explore cutting-edge tools, apps, and platforms that can revolutionize the way you handle your finances, saving you time, effort, and money.

We delve into the world of personal finance apps that help you track your expenses, set financial goals, and automate your budgeting process. We introduce you to advanced budgeting software that offers insightful analytics and visualization tools to monitor your financial progress effectively.

Furthermore, we discuss the advantages of online banking, electronic bill payment systems, and digital wallets, showcasing their convenience and security features. By embracing these technological advancements, you can optimize your financial management practices and stay ahead in today's fast-paced world.

7.5 Seeking Professional Advice for Wealth Management

WHILE EMPOWERING YOURSELF with knowledge is crucial, seeking professional advice is equally important for comprehensive wealth management. In this section, we emphasize the value of collaborating with financial experts who can provide personalized guidance tailored to your specific financial goals.

We explain how to choose the right financial advisor or wealth manager who aligns with your values and understands your aspirations. We outline the benefits of working with professionals who have a proven track record in investment management, retirement planning, and risk assessment.

By developing a strong relationship with a trusted financial advisor, you can access valuable insights, gain access to exclusive investment opportunities, and receive ongoing support to optimize your financial strategy. This section will equip you with the knowledge and confidence to embark on a successful partnership with a skilled professional who can help you navigate the complexities of wealth management.

In Chapter 7, we equip you with a comprehensive set of strategies for financial optimization. By implementing effective budgeting techniques, minimizing debt, leveraging tax planning strategies, embracing technology, and seeking professional advice, you will be well on your way to achieving financial prosperity, creating a secure future, and realizing your dreams. It is time to take control of your finances and embark on a journey towards a brighter financial future.

Chapter 8: Scaling and Maintaining Your Million-Dollar Empire

8.1 Strategies for Scaling a Successful Business Venture

In this chapter, we embark on an exciting journey of scaling your business venture to new heights. Scaling is a critical phase that requires careful planning, innovative strategies, and a visionary mindset. We will explore proven techniques that successful entrepreneurs have employed to expand their empires and achieve extraordinary growth.

Imagine taking your business from a local success story to a global phenomenon. It all starts with setting ambitious yet attainable goals. By defining clear objectives and developing a roadmap, you can chart a course towards exponential growth. We will delve into the art of strategic planning, identifying untapped markets, and leveraging cutting-edge technologies to gain a competitive edge.

Example: Let us take the example of "LuxeLife," a luxury fashion brand that began as a boutique in a small town. Through strategic partnerships, aggressive marketing campaigns, and an unwavering commitment to quality, LuxeLife expanded its reach to major cities worldwide. By consistently analyzing consumer trends and adapting to market demands, they built a recognizable brand that resonated with affluent clientele across the globe.

8.2 Building a Strong Team and Delegating

Responsibilities

NO EMPIRE CAN BE BUILT alone. In this section, we explore the importance of assembling a high-performing team and effectively delegating responsibilities. Surrounding yourself with talented individuals who share your vision and complement your skills is crucial to sustaining growth.

We will delve into the art of talent acquisition, nurturing a positive company culture, and fostering innovation within your team. By empowering your employees, encouraging their professional development, and providing them with the resources they need, you can create a workforce that is passionate, dedicated, and aligned with your business goals.

Example: "TechSolutions" began as a tech startup founded by a visionary entrepreneur. By carefully selecting individuals with diverse expertise and fostering a collaborative work environment, TechSolutions developed groundbreaking products and attracted top-tier clients. The company's success can be attributed to the founder's ability to identify and cultivate exceptional talent, resulting in a team that consistently delivered cutting-edge solutions.

8.3 Diversifying Investments for Long-Term Stability

TO BUILD A MILLION-dollar empire, you must not only focus on your core business but also explore opportunities for diversification. In this section, we explore the importance of diversifying investments to ensure long-term stability and sustainable growth.

We will discuss various investment vehicles, such as real estate, stocks, bonds, and alternative investments, which can help you grow and protect your wealth. By spreading your investments across different asset classes and industries, you can mitigate risks and create a resilient financial portfolio.

Example: "Global Ventures" is a conglomerate that started as a technology company but expanded into diverse sectors such as real estate, energy, and hospitality. By intelligently diversifying their investments, they were able to weather economic downturns, capitalize on emerging markets, and achieve consistent financial growth.

8.4 Adapting to Market Trends and Capitalizing on Opportunities

TO MAINTAIN YOUR EMPIRE'S momentum, it is crucial to stay ahead of market trends and seize opportunities as they arise. In this section, we explore the importance of adaptability, agility, and staying informed about the ever-evolving business landscape.

We will delve into market research techniques, competitive analysis, and the art of identifying untapped niches. By embracing innovation, embracing technology, and anticipating customer needs, you can position your business as a market leader and capitalize on emerging trends.

Example: "EcoSolutions" started as a small eco-friendly product company but quickly recognized the rising demand for sustainable solutions. By pivoting their product line to meet market needs, they became pioneers in the green technology sector, achieving exponential growth and industry recognition.

8.5 Maintaining a Wealthy Mindset and Giving Back to Society

TRUE SUCCESS IS NOT just measured by financial achievements but also by the impact you make on society. In this final section, we explore the importance of maintaining a wealthy mindset and giving back to the community that supports your empire.

We will delve into the power of positive thinking, gratitude, and philanthropy. By adopting a mindset of abundance and embracing social responsibility, you can create a lasting legacy and inspire others to reach for their dreams.

Example: "EmpowerEd" is a multimillion-dollar education company that believes in giving back. Through scholarships, mentorship programs, and educational initiatives in underserved communities, they have made a profound difference in the lives of countless students, empowering them to achieve their academic and professional goals.

Conclusion:

Scaling and maintaining a million-dollar empire requires strategic planning, a strong team, diversified investments, adaptability, and a wealthy mindset. By implementing the strategies outlined in this chapter, you can unlock new levels of success, achieve exponential growth, and leave a lasting impact on the world. It is time to take the reins of your empire and embark on a journey of limitless possibilities.

Chapter 9: Conclusion

9.1 Setting Realistic Expectations

In this concluding chapter, we delve into the importance of setting realistic expectations on your path to success. While it is essential to dream big and aim high, it is equally vital to ground those aspirations in reality. By setting realistic expectations, you create a solid foundation for your journey towards achieving your goals.

To set realistic expectations, take a holistic approach. Evaluate your current circumstances, resources, and abilities. Consider your strengths and weaknesses and identify the areas where you need to grow and develop. By understanding your starting point, you can chart a course that aligns with your capabilities and propels you towards progress.

9.2 Embracing a Growth Mindset

A GROWTH MINDSET IS a transformative tool that empowers you to embrace challenges, learn from setbacks, and continuously improve. In this section, we explore the power of adopting a growth mindset and its role in your journey towards success.

With a growth mindset, you view obstacles as opportunities for growth rather than roadblocks. You understand that failures are steppingstones to success and that every setback brings valuable lessons. By cultivating a growth mindset, you unlock your potential, unleash your creativity, and develop resilience, allowing you to overcome any obstacles that come your way.

9.3 Leveraging Compound Interest and Investments

THE POWER OF COMPOUND interest and investments cannot be overstated. In this section, we deep dive into the potential of leveraging compound interests to accelerate your wealth growth.

Compound interest is like a snowball rolling downhill, gaining momentum and size over time. By investing wisely and reinvesting your returns, you set in motion a cycle of exponential growth. As your investments compound, your wealth multiplies, creating a passive income stream that works tirelessly for you.

9.4 Exploring High-Risk, High-Reward Opportunities

WHILE THERE ARE RISKS involved, high-risk, high-reward opportunities can be a game-changer on your journey towards success. In this section, we explore the thrilling realm of taking calculated risks to achieve extraordinary outcomes.

High-risk, high-reward ventures require careful research, analysis, and risk management. By identifying opportunities with significant potential returns, you challenge yourself to step outside your comfort zone and embrace uncertainty. These ventures can yield remarkable rewards, propelling you towards your goals faster than you ever imagined.

9.5 Harnessing the Power of Entrepreneurship

ENTREPRENEURSHIP HOLDS boundless potential for those seeking to forge their own path to success. In this section, we embark on a visionary exploration of the transformative power of entrepreneurship.

By embracing entrepreneurship, you become the captain of your own ship, navigating uncharted waters towards unbounded possibilities. Entrepreneurship allows you to pursue your passions, create innovative solutions, and shape your own destiny. Through entrepreneurial ventures, you have the opportunity to leave a lasting impact on the world while building wealth and personal fulfillment.

9.6 Taking Advantage of Market Trends and Timing

TIMING IS EVERYTHING, and being coordinated with market trends can give you a significant advantage. In this section, we uncover the art of identifying and capitalizing on market trends to maximize your success.

By staying informed, conducting market research, and monitoring industry dynamics, you position yourself to seize opportunities as they arise. Understanding emerging trends allows you to adapt, innovate, and position yourself ahead of the curve, gaining a competitive edge in your chosen field.

9.7 Building a Strong Support Network

SUCCESS IS RARELY ACHIEVED in isolation. In this section, we emphasize the importance of cultivating a strong support network to propel you forward on your journey.

Surround yourself with like-minded individuals who share your vision and values. Cultivate relationships with mentors, advisors, and peers who can offer guidance, support, and inspiration. A strong support network provides encouragement during challenging times, celebrates your victories, and provides valuable insights and connections.

9.8 Celebrating Milestones and Staying Motivated

THROUGHOUT YOUR JOURNEY, it is crucial to celebrate milestones and maintain unwavering motivation. In this final section, we emphasize the importance of acknowledging your achievements and sustaining your drive.

Celebrate both small and significant milestones along the way. Acknowledge your progress and take the time to appreciate how far you have come. By celebrating your successes, you reinforce your motivation and inspire yourself to keep pushing towards greater heights.

Conclusion:

As we conclude this transformative journey, remember to set realistic expectations, embrace a growth mindset, leverage compound interest and investments, explore high-risk, high-reward opportunities, harness the power of entrepreneurship, take advantage of market trends and timing, build a strong support network, and celebrate milestones. With unwavering determination, resilience, and a clear vision, you have the power to shape your destiny and achieve extraordinary success. Embrace the journey ahead with energy, motivation, and unwavering belief in your limitless potential. Your future awaits, and it is filled with endless possibilities.

Chapter 10 (Bonus Chapter): A Step -by-Step Example on how to achieve the Million Dollar Goal

10.1 Real Example on How to Accomplish the Goal

Let us delve into the inspiring story of Sarah, an individual who dared to dream big and embarked on an extraordinary journey to transform $100 into a remarkable $1,000,000 within a single year. As we follow Sarah's steps, you will witness the power of determination, strategic planning, and calculated risk-taking.

10.2 Identifying High-Potential Investment Opportunities

SARAH'S QUEST BEGAN with meticulous research and only one hundred dollars, as she scoured the investment landscape for high-potential opportunities. She recognized that to achieve her ambitious goal, she needed to identify emerging industries and sectors with significant growth prospects. Sarah was drawn to the renewable energy sector, captivated by its potential for transformative change and sustainable returns. She also recognized the incredible growth potential of technology startups and the disruptive force of cryptocurrencies.

Undeterred by the inherent risks, Sarah dived into extensive analysis and due diligence. She evaluated companies, technologies, and market trends, seeking out the most promising investment vehicles within these sectors. Through her dedicated research, she unearthed hidden gems and identified opportunities that aligned perfectly with her risk appetite and financial goals.

10.3: Creating a Comprehensive Strategic Investment Plan

ARMED WITH HER NEWFOUND knowledge, Sarah embarked on the creation of a comprehensive strategic investment plan. She understood that success would require a meticulous approach, taking into account every detail and contingency. With passion and determination, Sarah laid out a step-by-step blueprint that would serve as her guiding light throughout the year.

In her plan, Sarah outlined specific milestones and timelines, providing a clear path to achieving her ultimate goal. She carefully considered capital allocation, strategically diversifying her investments across multiple opportunities. Recognizing the importance of managing risk, she developed exit strategies for each investment, ensuring she could capitalize on gains or mitigate losses along the way.

Sarah's plan was not just a rigid set of guidelines. It was a flexible framework that allowed her to adapt to changing market conditions, seize unforeseen opportunities, and make informed decisions. This dynamic approach ensured that she remained agile and responsive in an ever-evolving investment landscape.

By developing this strategic investment plan, Sarah set herself up for success. It provided her with a sense of direction, purpose, and confidence. Every decision she made was rooted in her plan, giving her the clarity and conviction necessary to navigate the challenging and volatile terrain of investing.

Sarah's real-life example demonstrates the incredible possibilities that lie within the realm of investment and financial growth. Through her unwavering determination, meticulous research, and strategic planning, she transformed a humble sum of $100 into an awe-inspiring $1,000,000 within a single year. Her journey is a testament to the power of setting audacious goals, pursuing knowledge, and taking calculated risks.

Example of Sarah's Investment Strategic Investment Plan

We will dive into Sarah's journey as she crafted a comprehensive strategic investment plan to identify emerging market business opportunities. With her audacious goal of turning $100 into an astounding $1 million within a single year, Sarah understood the importance of meticulous planning, calculated risk-taking, and a visionary mindset. Join us as we explore the key steps, she took to develop her plan, and let her example inspire you to create your own path to financial success.

1. Clarify Your Investment Objectives:

To begin, Sarah took the time to clarify her investment objectives. She asked herself essential questions, such as:

- What is my desired financial goal?

- What level of risk am I comfortable with?

- How much time and effort am I willing to dedicate to achieve my goal?

By gaining a clear understanding of her objectives, Sarah set the foundation for her strategic investment plan.

2. Research and Identify Emerging Market Business Opportunities:

Sarah was well aware that identifying emerging market business opportunities would be key to achieving her lofty financial target. She immersed herself in extensive research, studying market trends, industry reports, and expert analysis. She closely monitored emerging sectors, such as renewable energy, fintech, biotechnology, and artificial intelligence, seeking out companies with disruptive potential.

Within these sectors, Sarah identified specific businesses that demonstrated robust growth prospects, strong management teams, and innovative products or services. She conducted in-depth due diligence, analyzing financial statements, evaluating competitive advantages, and assessing market demand. Through this meticulous process, she unearthed high-potential investment opportunities that aligned with her risk appetite and financial goals.

3. Diversify Your Investment Portfolio:

Recognizing the importance of diversification, Sarah structured her strategic investment plan to include a well-balanced portfolio. She allocated her capital across multiple emerging market opportunities to spread risk and capture potential upside. By investing in various industries, she minimized the impact of any single investment's performance on her overall portfolio.

Sarah carefully considered the optimal allocation percentages for each investment, factoring in potential returns, associated risks, and her own risk tolerance. She sought a balance between higher-risk, higher-reward opportunities, and more stable investments to ensure a resilient portfolio.

4. Develop Entry and Exit Strategies:

Sarah understood that successful investments require both entry and exit strategies. She developed clear guidelines for entering into investment opportunities and criteria for knowing when to exit.

For entry, Sarah established specific indicators that signaled an opportune time to invest, such as a certain valuation, market milestones, or positive industry developments. These indicators ensured that she entered investments at favorable prices and with confidence in their growth potential.

Equally important were her exit strategies. Sarah set predefined criteria for selling her investments, including target profit levels, potential risks reaching a certain threshold, or changes in market dynamics. These strategies allowed her to secure gains and protect her capital from significant downturns.

5. Continuously Monitor and Adjust:

Sarah recognized that the investment landscape is ever evolving, and she embraced the need for continuous monitoring and adjustment. She closely tracked the performance of her investments, staying updated on market trends, news, and industry developments. This proactive approach allowed her to make informed decisions and adjust her investment plan accordingly.

By staying connected to the market, Sarah was able to identify new emerging opportunities and act swiftly when necessary. She remained agile, adapting her investment strategy based on real-time information and changing market conditions.

Conclusion:

Sarah's journey to turning $100 into $1 million within a year exemplifies the power of a comprehensive strategic investment plan. Through thorough research, diversification, well-defined entry and exit strategies, and continuous monitoring, she maximized her potential for success in emerging market business opportunities.

10.4 Leveraging Compound Interest and Investment Returns

SARAH UNDERSTOOD THE power of compound interest and the significant role it plays in wealth accumulation. She strategically reinvested any returns generated from her initial investments, allowing her capital to grow exponentially over time. By harnessing the compounding effect, Sarah maximized the potential returns on her investments.

10.5 Implementing Risk Management Strategies

RECOGNIZING THE INHERENT risks associated with investing, Sarah implemented robust risk management strategies. She diversified her portfolio across various asset classes and investment vehicles to mitigate potential losses. Additionally, she set clear stop-loss limits and employed thorough due diligence before committing her capital to any investment opportunity.

10.6 Harnessing the Power of Diversification

SARAH UNDERSTOOD THE importance of diversification in managing risk and maximizing returns. She carefully allocated her capital across a range of investments, including stocks, bonds, real estate, and alternative assets. This diversification strategy helped Sarah to minimize the impact of any underperforming investments while capitalizing on high-growth opportunities.

10.7 Maximizing Profit with Active Monitoring and Adjustments

SARAH ACTIVELY MONITORED her investments, staying informed about market trends and developments. She regularly reviewed her portfolio's performance and made necessary adjustments based on changing market conditions. By maintaining a proactive stance, Sarah capitalized on emerging opportunities and protected her portfolio from potential downturns.

10.8 Utilizing Technology and Tools for Investment Analysis

TO MAKE INFORMED INVESTMENT decisions, Sarah leveraged cutting-edge technology and analytical tools. She utilized robust investment platforms, market analysis software, and data-driven research tools to identify potential opportunities and evaluate their viability. This technological advantage provided Sarah with valuable insights, enabling her to make informed investment choices.

10.9 Overcoming Challenges and Staying Motivated

THROUGHOUT HER JOURNEY, Sarah encountered challenges and setbacks. However, she remained resilient and focused on her goal. She maintained a positive mindset, seeking inspiration from success stories of renowned investors and entrepreneurs. Sarah continually reminded herself of her purpose and the life-changing potential that awaited her at the end of the journey.

10.10 Celebrating Milestones and Successes

SARAH RECOGNIZED THE importance of celebrating milestones and successes along the way. As she achieved significant milestones and experienced profitable returns, she took the time to acknowledge and reward herself. Celebrating these successes provided her with the motivation and enthusiasm to continue pursuing her ambitious goal.

10.11 The Importance of Continual Learning and Adaptation

SARAH UNDERSTOOD THAT success in the investment world requires continual learning and adaptation. She remained committed to expanding her knowledge through books, seminars, and networking with industry professionals. By staying updated on market trends and evolving investment strategies, Sarah positioned herself to seize new opportunities and adjust her approach accordingly.

10.12 Scaling Up: Replicating Success for Future Endeavors

AS SARAH ACCOMPLISHED her goal of turning $100 into $1,000,000, she recognized the potential for further growth and success. Armed with invaluable experience, she replicated her successful strategies for future endeavors. Sarah embarked on new investment projects, building upon her previous achievements, and setting her sights on even greater financial milestones.

Conclusion:

Sarah's remarkable journey from $100 to $1,000,000 in one year serves as an inspiring real-life example of what can be achieved with determination, strategic planning, risk management, diversification, continuous learning, and adaptability. By following her steps and applying the principles discussed in this chapter, readers can embark on their own transformative journeys toward financial success. Remember, it is the combination of visionary thinking, meticulous execution, and unwavering motivation that can turn impossible goals into extraordinary realities.

As you embark on your own investment journey, let Sarah's example inspire you to develop your strategic plan with clarity, determination, and a visionary mindset. Remember to research diligently, seek diversification, and remain adaptable. With a well-crafted plan and unwavering commitment, you too can seize emerging market opportunities and achieve remarkable financial growth.

Don't miss out!

Visit the website below and you can sign up to receive emails whenever BRIAN MICHAEL LAWSON publishes a new book. There's no charge and no obligation.

https://books2read.com/r/B-A-DDBZ-ERSKC

BOOKS 2 READ

Connecting independent readers to independent writers.

Did you love *How to Turn One Hundred Dollars into One Million Dollars in One Year: A Guide to Exponential Wealth Creation*? Then you should read *Happily Ever After Is for You Too! A Guide to Never Giving Up Until You Find Your True Love*[1] by BRIAN MICHAEL LAWSON!

[2]

Happily Ever After Is for You Too! A Guide to Never Giving Up Until You Find Your True Love is an inspiring and uplifting book that offers hope and guidance to those who are searching for their perfect partner in life. With a heartfelt blend of personal anecdotes, practical advice, and insightful wisdom, this book empowers readers to persevere in their quest for love, reminding them that true love is not just reserved for fairy tales but is attainable for everyone. Through its pages, readers will discover valuable strategies for navigating the ups and downs of dating, building self-confidence, overcoming obstacles, and ultimately creating a

---

1. https://books2read.com/u/mK7GwB

2. https://books2read.com/u/mK7GwB

fulfilling and lasting relationship. With its warm and encouraging tone, this book serves as a beacon of light, reminding readers that their own happily ever after is within reach and inspiring them to never give up on the journey towards finding their one true love.

Also by BRIAN MICHAEL LAWSON

Thriving through Divorce: A Comprehensive Guide to Emotional,
Personal, and Financial Recovery
The Memory of Water
La Memoria del Agua
¡Cómo convertir $100 en $1,000,000 en 1 año! Una guía para la
creación de riqueza exponencial
Triunfando a Pesar del Divorcio: Una Guía Integral para la
Recuperación Emocional, Personal y Financiera
Happily Ever After Is for You Too! A Guide to Never Giving Up Until
You Find Your True Love
¡Y Fueron Felices Para Siempre también es para Ti! Una guía para
nunca rendirse hasta encontrar tu amor verdadero
Mujeres Bellas Denegadas
Girls Disavowed
How to Turn One Hundred Dollars into One Million Dollars in One
Year: A Guide to Exponential Wealth Creation

About the Author

Brian Michael Lawson is a published author (*The Memory of Water, Happily Ever After Is for You Too, Thriving Through Divorce,* and other titles). He is also an entrepreneur, engineer, and a content creator. He has been a senior manager for regional humanitarian project for the United Nations. He has an MBA degree and a Bachelor of Science Degree in Engineering.

www.ingramcontent.com/pod-product-compliance
Lightning Source LLC
Chambersburg PA
CBHW031124160726

47989CB00016B/1325